AWAKENING THE SOUL

A Practical Guide to Spiritual Growth

VINICIO SANCHEZ

Author's Tranquility Press
ATLANTA, GEORGIA

Copyright © 2024 by Vinicio Sanchez

All rights reserved. No part of this publication may be reproduced, distributed or transmitted in any form or by any means, including photocopying, recording, or other electronic or mechanical methods, without the prior written permission of the publisher, except in the case of brief quotations embodied in critical reviews and certain other noncommercial uses permitted by copyright law. For permission requests, write to the publisher, addressed "Attention: Permissions Coordinator," at the address below.

Vinicio Sanchez/Author's Tranquility Press
3900 N Commerce Dr. Suite 300 #1255
Atlanta, GA 30344, USA
www.authorstranquilitypress.com

Ordering Information:
Quantity sales. Special discounts are available on quantity purchases by corporations, associations, and others. For details, contact the "Special Sales Department" at the address above.

Awakening the Soul: A Practical Guide to Spiritual Growth/Vinicio Sanchez
Library of Congress Control Number: 2024918494
Hardback: 978-1-965463-07-9
Paperback: 978-1-964810-64-5
eBook: 978-1-964810-33-1

CONTENTS

Finding Your Truth i

PART 1 DEFINE SPIRITUALITY

Chapter 1: Define Spirituality 1
Chapter 2: Reality 5
Chapter 3: Perspective & Attitude 10
Chapter 4: Paradigm 13
Chapter 5: Character 23
Chapter 6: Mind & Consciousness 27
Chapter 7: Spirituality 33

PART 2 THE THREE DISCIPLINES

Chapter 8: The First Discipline - The Goal 38
The Second Discipline – Lead Measures 40
The Third Discipline – Reconcile 41
Chapter 9: Why? 42
Chapter 10: The Sample 44

Finding Your Truth

This book was created with the intention to help people find a way to spirituality. Nevertheless, this is only one of many ways that already exist, so do not take this as the ultimate or the only way. This is merely an attempt to formalize the way to spirituality.

This book came to me as an idea to standardize the spiritual realities, to make it simple to understand and simple to follow by using simple clear cut instructions. This to me is something very personal that I created for myself. I thought of this because I was trying to figure out a way that will lead me to my ultimate spiritual goal. I was yearning for finding a way and the way was shown to me.

The book is distributed in two parts and three main disciplines.

Part 1. Define Spirituality

Part 2. The Three Disciplines

1. Define Spiritual Goal
2. Lead measures
3. Reconcile

Again, this book is only one way of many, so this might not work for everyone.

PART 1: DEFINE SPIRITUALITY

Chapter 1: Define Spirituality

If you truly want to define you spiritual goal, you first need to define what spirituality is. So let's start by asking WHAT IS SPIRITUALITY?

You might want to begin by asking yourself the following questions to better comprehend and discern you understanding in regards to the definition of spirituality. Is important that you are honest and take the necessary time to answer them.

1. What do you know about Spirituality?
2. What does that mean to you?
3. Have you define its true meaning?

If you cannot answer these questions, then you might want to start there before you can move on to defining your spiritual goal.

For many spirituality is, something mystical, nonmaterial, something that cannot be proved, that cannot be touched, seen, or heard. That for one to be spiritual one must be separated from our material desires.

Others think of spirituality in terms of religious ceremonies, rituals, chanting, divine, and sacred. That one must be part of a faith in order to be spiritual. They would claim that spirituality is related to the spirit of God, but what is the Spirit of God? It all sounds very ambiguous to many of us.

The definition from the Old Testament states that "the spirit of God is the breath of God, is the force that gives life to man", but what is this breath or this force? The New Testament states that "the Spirit is the power that will create eternal life", but what is this power? Some say that this power is given by the Spirit of The Lord Jesus Christ, and that by accepting The Lord Jesus Christ in your heart you will receive this power or spirit.

These answers to me are still unclear and do not explain what this power or spirit is. So, what is this spirit?

That is where we need to start. We need to start by asking the tough questions. There is nothing wrong with questioning, we are not doubting the existence of spirituality or God for that matter. We are merely trying to understand its true and deep meaning.

We are very well aware of our physical reality, we live it every day and seem to understand it at least in a deeper sense compare to spirituality. The spiritual reality is complicated to explain and to understand for the human mind, because of its mystical, nonphysical realities, and because spirituality defies the human physical senses and cannot be proven by any physical reactions, at least in the current accepted standard scientific methods.

Though, there are scientist now days that are starting to theorize about this reality and its implications in modern science. These new fields of study are, The String Theory, The Hologram Universe Theory, and Quantum Mechanics and its connections to Consciousness. For example, in Quantum Mechanics there is the most famous experiment that shows how individual particles when not observed behaved like a wave and when observed behaved like particles. Showing that the observer influences all physical reality, that all possibilities are present without the observer and that all possibilities collapse to one once the observer is present. This means that depending on what you, belief to be truth or real, you will experience only one possibility. We decide which possibility we experience consciously or unconsciously. This makes me wonder about how reality really works and how we can apply this into our daily lives. But to avoid getting away from the matter of spirituality I will not go into detail on the previously mentioned subjects. I do recommend that you do your own research and find out more about them.

Spirituality can be many things depending on the perspective of everyone. Many could say that spirituality is sacred, that is something only saints and mystics can understand. Others might say that it's a mystical, and an abstract reality out of reach of human understanding. So, the next question is, where do we start?

Well, the answer is within your grasp, is not far. The answer is within. You do not need to learn the meaning of spirituality, you simply need to remember, to look within, within your personal experience.

Nonetheless, even when we look within, we get lost and we are not able to discern the truth. Looking within is a challenge for many of us, since this is something, we practice very little to none in our lives, but it is achievable.

Besides, we need to consider that spirituality cannot be explained in one word, or paragraph, or book for that matter. Spirituality is difficult to describe with human words, but that is not the only reason. Let me explain why.

Imagine you have met someone who has never seen the sun, or has smelled a rose, and you want to describe those experiences to that person. How can you describe the magnificent view of the daylight or the delicious aroma of the rose to someone who has never seen the sun or smelled a rose? Take a moment to think about it.

You can try and try and maybe compare them to similar experiences to try to describe them to that person, but that individual will never fully grasp both experiences unless he or she personally experiences these events themselves.

The same goes for spiritual realities. How can I explain something so magnificent, so beautiful, and so delightful, to someone who has never experienced Spirituality or is not aware of its existence?

Nevertheless, I will try. For those who know the answer, or have experienced and understand the spiritual world, can skip this step and move on to defining the 'Spiritual Goal'. But those who need more guidance can stay with me. However, I will not only try to describe it, but I will also show you the way to experience it. But for that to happen, it's going to require me to talk about a few other subjects to better illustrate the meaning of Spirituality. At least what I have come to understand.

The first subject I want to talk about is Reality and its connection to our mind. As we go on to the next chapter, we will discuss the connection between Perspective and Attitude.

In addition to the previous chapter, I will elaborate more on Perspective and Attitude and its connections to our mental Paradigms and Character.

In the next chapter, we will go into further discussion about the inner dimensions of the Mind and Consciousness. As we go on, we will finally conclude part one of the book with the meaning of Spirituality.

This is an attempt to outline its meaning in modern terms. It might not be perfect or complete, but this is what I have come to understand from my personal experience. We need to understand that what I'm about to describe is complicated and is being described from one point of reference and its description might be incomplete. Is always important to question what is being said here. So, let's dive in and take the chance to learn something new.

Chapter 2: Reality

Many of us go through life without ever taking the time to notice the different aspects of our reality and some of us are only focused on one part of that. This is a situation which has resulted in the establishment of different groups that have tried to describe our reality. As a result, today we have scientists, philosophers, and religionists as part of these main groups. These groups have tried to understand and have tried to find the truth about our reality, but none have succeeded.

Science focuses on the mechanics of the universe, religion focuses on the doctrines of a group and faith, and philosophy focuses only in logic and theory. All three seem to be describing something different and not related from one to another. They seemed to be describing different realities that are far apart from each other. Though, in truth all three describe a different part of the whole.

Unfortunately, some people think that science is the only path to describe, understand, and find the truth about our reality. Others think that religion is the only one with all the truth and knowledge. And very few think philosophy is the way. Thus, this current approach is very limiting for the full understanding of our reality. It seems to be giving us different descriptions and facts of something that we experience every day. Consequently, creating confusion, a limiting and distorted picture of what we see and experience in our everyday lives.

We cannot answer all questions by only focusing on one part of the whole. This present approach provides a very narrow and limiting view of the universe. It reminds me of an old Indian story of five blind men and an elephant, where the five blind men are trying to describe the elephant by touch to each other, but each described something very different from the other.

The story goes something like this. There was an elephant and there were five blind men in a room. The five men were trying to describe the elephant by touch. One was touching the tail, another one was touching the elephant's trunk, the third one was touching the midsection, the fourth one was touching one leg, and the last one was touching the elephant's ear. All five-man had different descriptions of the elephant. The first one described it as a rope, the second one as a snake, the third one as a wall, the fourth one described it as a pillar, and the last one as a sail. This of course created disagreement between the five blind men. They argued about how wrong the other was, not realizing that they were describing a part of the elephant and not that entire elephant.

The same is happening with our religion, science, and philosophy. Each group believes to have the most accurate view of our reality. As the five-blind man, our scientist, religionist, and philosophers share the same dilemma. Their view of the universe is incomplete and narrow. They are failing to see the whole picture.

Our science is only focused on describing the part of our reality that we can experience with our physical senses, but ignores the part that we experience with our inner-feelings, thoughts, and consciousness.

Our religions are focus only on our feelings and beliefs, but completely ignores the facts of what we experience with our physical senses and consciousness.

Our philosophers focus on consciousness, and meaning, but ignore our feelings, and faith.

Neither of them seems to understand that each is describing an important part of our reality. Thus, taking us further to confusion and to a limiting view of the universe.

Hence, to reach a complete view and understanding of our reality we must consider each other's perspective and experiences. We must understand that our reality is composed of the physical world, the mind, and the spirit. Categories which compose one whole or in other words our reality. If one of the three is taken to the extreme without understanding or considering the other, the results can be misleading and limited, therefore, ending up with what we currently have. Therefore, we must accept that there is more and that we are missing out on the opportunity to see more and understand more if we only focus our attention on only one side of our entire reality.

We must accept that anything that has being created was first a thought. Everything started as an idea. This idea then moved to word, then moved to deed. Therefore, "that of which you think of, but never speak of, creates at one level. That which you think of and speak of creates at another level. That which you think, speak, and do becomes made manifest in your reality" by Neal Donald Waltch from his book Conversations with God.

We experience this in our everyday lives. The cellphone that we tirelessly use every day was first an idea. The coffee or breakfast you made this morning first came to you as an idea. The coffee came to your experience by using the three levels of reality, so does everything else you do or create. Your job, your career, your relationships, your failures, and successes. The sum of all is your current reality and all came to you first as a thought.

Is important to keep in mind that everything we think, say and do creates our reality. Doing without thinking is impossible. Even if the thinking was unconscious there still was an original thought. To better explain this, I like to use the example of a sandwich story I saw in a documentary that was trying to illustrate this process. It goes something like this; for the sandwich to come into existence, it had to first be an idea, a thought. A person had to think for a moment about eating a sandwich. Then, that person took upon that idea and created the sandwich.

Now, there are two levels of thinking when anything comes to mind, the unconscious thinking and the conscious thinking. The unconscious thinking usually starts with any type of feeling, then that feeling triggers a thought, then thought placed into action becomes reality.

In the other hand, the conscious thinking happens in a very different way. In this kind of situation, the person becomes aware of the first thought or feeling and decides to think of something else. For instance, instead of acting on the thought of making a sandwich or the feeling of wanting to eat a sandwich one can stop and think about that option and maybe bring a second option purposely, perhaps a more educated one, a well thought idea, possibly one with purpose. One can think of a sandwich or think of a healthier and sustainable choice. It all depends at what level of consciousness we are doing it. We can come up with something better or worse for us.

The first example was to act on it quickly without giving it to much thinking, but the second option requires awareness, time, and effort. It requires thinking with purpose, with and end in mind. For example, one can be thinking about losing weight, if this is the case then the option might be one with less calories, less carbs, less meat, or something else, depending on what we are looking for to accomplish. We can also have a goal to reduce our carbon footprint in the world, so we decide to eat something more sustainable for the earth and still heathy for the body. This is the difference between those who live with purpose and those who don't.

Those who live with purpose have a purpose for everything they think about, everything they say, and do. All is well thought of. They never do something without first thinking about it and making a truly conscious decision before acting on it.

These types of individuals truly live their lives by self-design. They are aware of their thoughts. They understand that thoughts are just previews of what can be. They also understand the implications and consequences if they decide to act on them. They understand the law of cause and effect. They understand Newton's third law of motion, which also applies to what we think, say, and do in our everyday lives. This law states that "for every action there is an equal and opposite reaction". Such law is flawless and those who do not understand it will suffer the consequences and effects of their actions. Our thoughts, words and deeds are the cause that creates the reaction. The reactions can be either positive or negative, we simply must decide what kind of effect we want to experience. Some examples I can think of are the times when we forget to set up the clock to wake up earlier than usual, and as a result, we are late for our early appointment. Or the time when we worked hard, organized ourselves, dedicated the necessary time, and effort, and as a result, we are successful at meeting our goals.

In the other hand, there are others who would base their actions on what they believe is right or have learned from others to be right without thinking about the consequences of their decisions. This kind of thinking is composed of other levels of reality that we are not aware of, and that we will be discussing in our next chapters.

For now, let's recap what we have learned in this current chapter:

1. Our Reality cannot be described by only one group that describes one part of the WHOLE.
2. Our Reality is composed of three different levels, Thought, Word and Deed.
3. For every action there is an equal and opposite reaction.

Chapter 3: Perspective & Attitude

Perspective is a point of view, is a way of interpreting things and events. Perspective is one point of view of many possibilities. As individuals with individual minds, ideas and beliefs, we can only experience one part of any event from our point of reference. Our attitude is also responsible for how we experience things and how we describe them to others.

Haven't you noticed the days when you have a good attitude your day and life seems to be in harmony and beautiful, but the days you wake up in a bad mood things start to go wrong one after the other, frustrating you and upsetting you more?

The reason a group of people who witness an event can give different descriptions of it is due to their attitudes and perspective. Each of them had a limited perspective and each had a different attitude towards the event.

Perspective is the way we process the information we are given. Have you heard of the famous saying for describing different perspectives, "glass half empty or glass half full"?

Each of us experience things differently, some of us more negatively and others more positively and these are influence by our attitude.

Due to our limited view of our reality and our limited ability to process information we are subject to only experiencing a fraction of any event. This fragmental experience is also subject to the way we process the information we receive, which is related to our attitudes. Our attitude plays a great role in the way we process the information we are receiving, the way we look at things, events, and people.

Therefore, in order to change your perspective, you must change your attitude. One's attitude is what determines our success or failure in life. A person with a negative attitude will not be successful even if that person has prepared all his/her life to meet one goal. We see this very often with some professionals who study and prepared themselves to become great doctors, lawyers, businessmen, or engineers, but for some reason some tend to succeed, and others don't. Despite the fact that many have the same opportunities, same knowledge, same education, and preparation. However, many still believe that there are other important conditions that will determine one's success.

Many believe that some fail due to bad luck or poor connections and support. Those same people would think that your network will determine your success, others believe that is all about location and education. But the real reason some make it, and others don't, is simply because of their attitude. Those with a positive mental attitude tend to be more positive towards their challenges, lives, and their relationships with others. A person with a positive mental attitude will never see himself as a victim of others, will not look at challenges as impossible obstacles to overcome.

A person with a positive attitude will always see challenges as an opportunity to grow and learn something new. They will see failure as something learned.

A person with a positive attitude understands that "successful people are not people without problems; they are simply people who've learned to solve their problems" (Lead the Field by Earl Nightingale).

In the other hand, the person with a mental negative attitude will see any problem as a result of external circumstances. Any challenge becomes an impediment to getting what they want. Any problem big or small, real or not real, becomes something out of their control. A person with a negative mental attitude will blame others for their failures, or circumstances. They often do not see that is their thinking and doing that blocks their way to success. I know many people that will not decide because of fear. Fear of failure, fear of the unknown. But this is just an idea, and too often is not real.

I have known people that are distrustful of others and think everyone is out to get them. They do not trust anyone, even those who genuinely want to help them, thus they end up not getting the help they truly needed, and their suspicion becomes true.

Failure does not exist in the eyes of a person with a positive mental attitude. This is because a person with a positive mental attitude sees what others call failure or a possibility of failure, as an opportunity to learn something new. For them there are only two main outcomes to anything they set their minds to achieve. They either succeed in meeting their goal right away or they learn something new along the way before they meet their goal. For them to be successful is not a matter of possibility, rather a matter of time.

Perspective and attitude are also connected to our mental paradigm. In our next chapter, we will go into more detail about Paradigms, for now let's summarize what is in this chapter:

1. Perspective is a point of view, a way of experiencing things, and events.
2. Perspective is mainly driven by attitude.
3. We must change our attitude if we want to change our perspective.

Chapter 4: Paradigm

Our attitude to life greatly depends on our mental paradigms. According to Stephen R. Covey an American author and very successful businessman" A paradigm is an explanation of certain aspects of the territory-It is a theory, an explanation, or model of something else. We have theories or models in our minds that define the way we think things are (Realities) and theories of the way things should be (Values)".

We use these paradigms to interpret events, things, and people. We use them to make decisions for our everyday life. Our judgment and understanding of things are based on and filtered by these paradigms.

One personal experience that I can use as an example of how our mental paradigm can affect our perspective and attitude, is the day that seventeen of my employees were missing one full week of pay from their paycheck. Many of them were very upset including myself, we truly had a reason to be upset, this was not the first time that this had happened in a three-month period. And to make matters worse it was the last week of the month, bills needed to be paid, food to buy, etc. I was so upset that I decided to call the COO of the company to complain about the mistake. I was very upset with the payroll department. I stated very firmly how unacceptable this situation was, and how irresponsible and unprofessional the department was for letting this happen yet again. I asked the COO that something needed to change to prevent this from happening in the future. After complaining about the situation, I called the payroll department Manager to let her know about the problem. The payroll manager sounded very disappointed and frustrated when she learned about the situation. She told me that she was going to take care of it right away and overnight the checks. A few minutes later she called me back to tell me that she was not able to cut any checks because the hours were never approved by the property manager and that she could not do anything until this was done. Can you imagine what I felt at that moment? My paradigm changed from being quick to judge a situation based on my past experiences, to realizing that I was wrong, and I had to learn to first investigate before jumping to conclusions and treat each situation as a new event. Suddenly my perspective changed, and my attitude towards her and the situation changed.

Things like this tend to happen to many of us all the time. We frequently let our old ideas and old beliefs get in the way of our good judgment. We simply jump to conclusions and use our old paradigms to discern things and events, thus influencing how we feel, how we act, and our attitude.

A paradigm is better known as an expectation. Expectations are theories of how things should be. We have expectations of our family members, friends, and the world that surrounds us. We have theories in our minds on how things should be, how people should be, how the world should be, and we hold them to those expectations. If things or people do not meet our expectations, we get frustrated or disappointed. For instance, we might have a family member, such as an immature father or mother or an immature child, who makes us feel frustrated or disappointed, because they might not be behaving the way we think they should, This is the main reason relationships are difficult, because some of us hold people to a certain standard or expectation, and when they do not meet that standard or expectation, we cannot accept it and start protesting against it. We try to control them, try to change the situation, or the person, but that never works. We are left with two choices, we either accept it, change our paradigm and work around the situation so that it does not affect us directly, or we continue to struggle and try to make the situation or person meet our expectations.

Expectations are not bad, expectations are what sometimes makes us strive for a better world, to a better us. With that being said, we should apply our theories of how things should be to ourselves and strive to improve oneself and not others.

One can try to have a good attitude about a situation, a person, or a thing, but if our mental paradigm is composed of our old beliefs and ideas, then is going to be very difficult to maintain a positive attitude.

Think of a time in which you started a day with a positive mental attitude, but something happened, or someone did something that made you change your attitude. Maybe someone offended you, attacked you; maybe you had an accident, or caught up a flu. Many things could have happened that made you change your mood and made it difficult for you to maintain that positive attitude throughout the day. Maybe you tried to force yourself and encourage yourself to think that things were ok, that you should be positive despite the current circumstances. Yet, for some reason or another there was a little voice telling you that you were lying to yourself and that you should be upset instead, because things are not the way they should be. At that point, you go back to your old negative attitude and fail to maintain a positive outlook of things.

What is it then?

Why so many of us cannot seem to keep a positive attitude, but others seem to do so?

Is there something wrong with us?

What are we missing?

Is this just wishful thinking?

Many people struggle with this, in fact most of us do. When we try to have a positive attitude, life happens, and we lose it. This is not because we are not good at keeping a positive attitude or because this idea of positive thinking is an illusion, or a lie created by someone who believes in wishful thinking or because we are bad people. In fact, the reason we fail to maintain a positive attitude no matter the circumstances is because our mental paradigm is still made up of our old ideas, old values, old beliefs, our old expectations. We cannot change our attitude without first starting to change our old paradigms or get rid of them. As Jesus said it in the bible. "Truly, truly, I say to you, unless one is born again, he cannot see the kingdom of God" (John 3:3). When Jesus said this to the Pharisee, the Pharisee had asked how he can see the kingdom of God, and Jesus responded this way to show that we must start from zero. People will not be able to see things in a positive way unless they let go of their old paradigms. From a spiritual perspective, people will have to be reborn again to see things differently, just as Jesus suggested. This means letting go of any learned ideas, beliefs, and values.

Let's go back to our previous example where you were having a good day, but someone insulted you and you felt offended. As part of our paradigm, we tend to value what others think of us, thus the opinion of others towards us can have a great impact on our attitude. But the moment we change what we value; from what others think of us to what we think of ourselves. The insults or opinion of others will stop being of our concern, therefore allowing us to maintain a good attitude despite the circumstance.

Nonetheless, this is a difficult request for most of us. This means for many of us letting go of our identity, of who we think we are. Lose everything that we believe to be true and important in our lives. This we cannot do. Many of us will die first before letting go of our values. This is a big order and I completely understand. This too is very difficult for me.

Our fear of losing who we are is stronger than our frustrations and problems. Many of us would not let go of our "identity" and belief system. Many of these beliefs are part of our culture, heritage, nationality, and even race. Our parents taught us to follow their advice, their culture, and heritage as they did from their parents. Thus, we adopted their old paradigms and continue living as our ancestors did.

Many will say then, what is wrong with that?

The answer to that question is that there is nothing wrong with anything. That is not the question to ask here. The real questions to ask are:

1. Is all that you have learned serving you?
2. Is your culture and heritage serving you?
3. Are you joyful and delighted every day of your life?

If the answer is 'Yes' to all three questions. Then, you do not need to keep reading this book. You have found your spiritual goal and live a blissful life. But, if all answers are 'No', then you might need to let go of your fear and try something new.

We do what our well-intended parents taught us, and we continue to try to solve the same old problems over and over again without results by doing the same things our ancestors did before us. I believe Einstein called this insanity." Doing the same thing over and over again and expecting different results".

However, not all the old paradigms are necessarily bad or wrong, some of them are simply incomplete, just as the experiments from science, the beliefs from religion, and theories from philosophy. Most of these are describing an incomplete picture of reality, thus creating the incorrect paradigm.

Think of a paradigm as a map of a territory, think of your values, ideas and beliefs as the name of the streets, the directions, and coordinates of a city.

Now, think of this map as the map from New York and think of a person using it to navigate through the city of Tokyo. As you just realized this person is most likely going to get lost and frustrated very quickly for using the incorrect map. The same happens with us when we use the incorrect paradigm in our lives to navigate through our problems and daily challenges.

For some odd reason we continue to use the old paradigm to navigate through new territories even when we find ourselves frustrated and lost at the end. We see this frustration in today's world. Many people are frustrated with their government, the economy, and everything in general. But this is happening because a big group of people refuses to change their beliefs, values, and ideas and they keep trying to apply the old with the new. Unfortunately, change is inevitable, and we must accept that change is part of life, and to survive more graciously we must change too.

And to make matters even worse, we never question ourselves about possibly using the incorrect map. We do it once, we do it twice, and we do it as many times we can. Some of us believe that eventually something has to give in, that if we keep trying, we will get through. Unfortunately, just trying is not enough. We must get creative and try new things, in different ways to get the results we want.

One believe that I can think of that many people have today that is causing much frustration, is the general believe that things happen to them, and that they have nothing to do with their circumstances or do not have any control over them. Consequently, if you hold those beliefs, you will never be able to change your life towards where you want it to go, then is going to be very hard for you to keep a positive attitude. You cannot hold a positive attitude if you believe that things are happening to you. You will constantly blame others for the things that are happening around you. Then, you will be upset with them for "doing things to you". You will lose your positive attitude at the very moment something happens that you feel is not under your control.

How can one person hold a positive attitude if that person truly believes this is the truth?

Is fundamentally impossible. If one wants things to change, one must let go of that idea. One truly need to start from zero and be born again. In this case change one's paradigm from being the victim and not having control over what happens, to a paradigm where one is fully aware that every action has a reaction, and one is in control.

Instead of believing that villains, evil, and bad luck exist. We never stop to think that perhaps those are our own creations, and we imagine them to exist, so that we feel better about ourselves when things do not go our way. This way we can blame someone or something else for our failures.

We must realize that anything that happened, is happening, and will happen to us, is our own doing, is under our control. There is no villain out there trying to unambiguously harm you, and there is no such thing as bad luck. The only villain out there and your worst enemy is your own self, and bad luck is the result of your own actions collectively or individually.

The evil in the world is the result of our collective thinking and doing. Evil does not exist until someone or many of us make a decision that will have an unpleasant effect on others and sometime on ourselves.

Conversely, some of you might be thinking, what about that car accident that I did not cause? Well, I tell you this, even though the car accident might not be entirely your fault. The reality is that the moment you make the decision to adventure out in the streets and drive the car, you have put yourself at risk of being part of an accident.

Do not take this claim from me, take it from the NHTSA. According to the National Highway Traffic Safety Administration there are over thirty thousand fatal crashes every year in the United States. This means that there is a possible chance for anyone driving a car today of being part of a fatal car accident and losing their lives. Now this does not mean we should become paranoid and never do anything because of the risks, instead we should become aware of all the possibilities and that this has nothing to do with luck.

The same is with everything else you do. At some point in time, you made a choice consciously or unconsciously that created your current unpleasant or pleasant reality. The problem with this is that most people, when deciding, are not aware of all the possible outcomes.

We create our reality individually or collectively. The current wars, diseases, famine, injustice, and suffering in the world are the result of our collective choices. We choose our current world circumstances collectively and individually unconsciously or consciously.

I can hear some of you saying, 'well I have nothing to do with any of those'. But I can tell you that if you look close enough you will realize that you did something or you are doing something that promotes and supports these events. Our everyday choices, buying habits, political association, eating habits, and lifestyle, will always have a positive or negative effect in the world.

For example, eating meat contributes to deforestation, greenhouse gases, and climate change. Eating high amounts of meat can also lead to health issues, obesity, cancer, diabetes, heart disease, and sometimes death. We are not aware of all of these consequences when we are eating a hamburger, but the worst part is that when we get cancer for eating unhealthy food, we do not take any blame and we just blame it on what we often call "bad luck" or even God. Thus, every day we make the unconscious decision of eating unhealthy food and putting ourselves at risk of suffering many illnesses related to unhealthy eating.

The deforestation of the Amazon is a direct effect of our daily consumption of meat. Nonetheless, we do not accept any responsibility even though we buy meat almost every day from the very same producers who are destroying the Amazons to raise cattle. We support the destruction of the Amazons by buying the products from the very people who are destroying it. We are as guilty as they are. Change your eating habits and start supporting those producers who are not destroying the very things that keep us alive. Then, you will see the changes happening almost overnight. This is already happening with the new trend of people starting to change their lifestyle and becoming more conscious about their eating habits. In 2016 the American Cancer Society has reported a continued steady decline in cancer deaths in the United States, many which was attributed to healthy eating.

Similarly, there are many other things that we do every day that support the bad behaviors from others that create war, famine, suffering, injustice and all the things that we call "evil" in the world. Unfortunately, not until we realize that we are part of the problem and take some responsibility, these problems will never go away, and we will continue to suffer the consequences of our unconscious actions and decisions.

In regard to all these previous claims I invite you to do some research on your own to see how they are all connected. There are hundreds of studies that support these claims that have come from institutes such as the United Nations Foundation, the International Livestock Research Institute in Kenya, the Commonwealth Scientific and Industrial Research Organization (CSIRO) in Australia and the International Institute for Applied Systems Analysis (IIASA) in Australia, just to name a few.

Our paradigms are composed of a very complex networking of interconnected ideas, beliefs and values. It's a complicated network that would take years for anyone to disassemble and counter argue. My attempt in this chapter is not to take the enormous task of dismantling old paradigms, this is something each of us must do individually. My only true attempt is to make you think and question both what I'm stating and what you currently belief, thus starting the process of critical thinking, self-awareness, and responsibility.

In conclusion, our paradigm is composed of our beliefs, ideas and values. Those are the basis of our decisions on everything we think, say, and do. It all comes down to the knowledge (data) that we collect from others, and our own experiences. These paradigms are a clear representation of our Character and Spirituality. If you change your paradigm, you will change your perspective and attitude, then you will change your Character.

Let's summarize what we have learned in this chapter.

1. Our mental paradigm is composed of our ideas, beliefs, and values.
2. Change your ideas, beliefs, and values and you will change your paradigm, then your attitude and perspective.
3. Let go of all your old paradigms if you want to see things in a new way.

Chapter 5: Character

Character is the mental and moral qualities distinctive of an individual. These mental and moral qualities are the very foundation of our mental paradigms, attitudes, and perspectives. Character is the projection of our paradigms, perspective, and attitudes. A well-formed Character is vital for the success of an individual. Our character determines our living experience and our life's outcomes. Character is a way of living, a way of being, a way of doing, and a way of thinking.

The results that we acquire in life are in direct proportion of our Character. A person with a poor character will get poor results. In the other hand, a person with a well-formed character will get great result in life. We see this in our own personal experience, for instance, if we have a loving character towards others, we experience love from others towards us. If we have a character based on fear or hate, we experience hate or fear towards us from others.

We also see this happening when we have a confident character or doubtful character. When we are confident, and know what we are doing, things tend to go well or as planned. If an unexpected challenge comes across our confident mind will find a solution. A solution will be found just as if you were looking through the calm and clear waters of a shallow lake in which you can clearly see the bottom floor. When a person is confident their mind tends to remain calm, thus giving the person the ability to clearly see a solution to any problem.

In contrast, when we are doubtful and fearful our minds get clouded with thoughts of fear. And when things do not go as planned, we are filled with intense emotions that obstruct our decision-making process and rational thinking. Fear tends to cloud our minds and good judgment. Thus, preventing us from getting a solution that only a confident and calm mind would find. Researchers have found that fear increases the flow of hormones to the amygdala, while impairing other parts of the brain such as the hippocampus responsible for regulating emotions and long-term memory, thus interrupting our ability to regulate our emotions, impacting our decision making, leading us to intense emotions, and impulsive reactions (by the University of Minnesota).

The universe is an exact mirror of who we are as individuals. Our external experience mirrors our internal reality or in other words our Character determines our external reality.

One personal experience I can recall when my character had determined my external reality was with my wife. I have noticed that the days that I have acted with a very loving character towards her, her character was always of love towards me, but when I change my inner reality to that of impatient or angry, her character often mirrored that impatience and anger towards me. I have noticed that this can happen from one day to another or even on the same day.

Think of a time in which you have experienced something similar with your family, friends or even strangers. You will realize that everyone has mirrored who you were at that very moment. However, keep in mind that there are still those who will not have control of their character, and could act viciously even when you are calm. In those cases, our biggest challenge becomes our ability to control ourselves. I have experienced this myself with some clients, many times throughout my career I have dealt with clients that are very upset and overly aggressive towards me even when I had nothing to do with the reason they are upset, but they want to vent, and scream. Staying calm and quiet in these circumstances is a major challenge for me. Letting the client calm down on their own is not easy. Controlling oneself can be sometimes impossible.

We can only control ourselves, our thoughts, our words, and our actions. We can try to control others, but the reality is that we do not have the same influence on others as we do on ourselves.

Controlling our character consciously and with purpose is by itself the most difficult task any human can undertake. Think of the time in which someone attacked you, I'm sure that your reaction was to defend yourself and attack back. Most of us do, this is a very natural reaction well known by psychology as, the **fight-or-flight** response (also called hyperarousal', or the acute stress response) is a physiological reaction that occurs in response to a perceived harmful event, attack, or threat to survival, this was first described by Cannon, Walter (1932). *Wisdom of the Body.* We often react the same way others act towards us. Imagine trying to remain peaceful and calm in a situation in which you are being attacked. This is something that is impossible to do for most of us. So, do not attempt to change another's attitude, instead maintain and control your own. This is more important; this is challenging enough. Our attempt to change others is futile unless they are willing to change for themselves.

One of the reasons we have such a chaotic world today is because most of us do not have self-control. If all of us could accomplish a hundred percent self-control, there would be no conflict in the world today. Imagine if everyone was peaceful and calm, not looking for revenge or getting even. How would that look like?

Most of us live our lives on autopilot, always reacting to circumstances unconsciously, doing things mostly by instinct. This causes our reality to be like a ship would be without a captain on a vast ocean with storms and challenges along the way. A ship in such a situation will get nowhere purposely, it will get lost and if it gets anywhere it will only be by chance or it will most likely sink. What are the odds that a ship in the Pacific Ocean without a course in place can get to a specific destination by chance? One can say that it's almost impossible. That's exactly the situation in which we are currently living. We have no course, no control, and no destination." If you don't know where you're going, you could wind up someplace else" by Yogi Berra. We must choose what kind of people we want to be. There are three types of people; "some people make things happen, some people watch things happen, other people wonder what the heck happened".

We have no control of our character; therefore, we have no control of our circumstances and outcomes. Learn to control your character and you will find that your ship will no longer be moved by the currents of life without your permission.

Now let's recap this chapter:

1. Our external experience mirrors our internal experience
2. Our Character is comprised of our mental paradigms, attitudes, and perspectives.
3. Self-control is the highest challenge

Chapter 6: Mind & Consciousness

According to a mystic from India called Sadhguru there are four levels or dimensions of the mind that are composed of the Intellect, Identity, Memory, and Intelligence. These dimensions of the mind are responsible for how we process and experience our reality.

The dimension of the intellect is the one in which society has focused most of its energy and its efforts. Our entire education system is based on this level of the mind. We educate our children to become intellectual, to memorize terms, names, dates, rules, and processes. Every year more children learn to read at an earlier age than the previous year, but they are never taught to deal with conflict and resolution, self-identity, creativity, and critical thinking. Our young children and most adults do not know the true meaning of respect, integrity, responsibility, and fairness. Our educations system is mainly focused on creating human robots, human machines that only collect data and follow instructions. We ignore the other parts of the mind, and we invest very little on critical thinking, identity, and intelligence.

The dimension of Identity is where we struggle the most. Many of today's human suffering comes from this level. Many people suffer from lack of self-identity, and of belonging. This is something very deep and important in our experience, yet we do not spend any effort or resources to try to truly understand it.

According to a research we see more of these effects in our adolescents "whom during this stage they are faced with physical growth, sexual maturity, and new ideas of themselves and what others think of them". Thereby, adolescents undergo through the process of resolving their identity crisis without any support or real coaching from our society or school system. All wars, gangs, cults, racism, over exaggerated nationalism are symptoms of this problem. People have joined gangs, cults, and groups, in an attempt to find a place of belonging and self-identity. The main reason there is so much separation in the world is because of our failure to recognize the real problem, our failure to understand self-identity. We do not recognize it as an important part of our experience. We ignore it and place limits on it.

Some of the symptoms that we are experiencing today in this world are the hundreds of different religions that exist today, the race problems, our over exaggerated nationalism, and our indifference to world hunger and poverty.

We are lost in the matter of identity. We have created limits to our identity by placing labels and divisions between us and others. We have placed an invisible line that separates us from others and even from the world that feeds us and takes care of us. We have lost our true boundless identity in exchange for a limited one. Thus, creating the illusion of separation, allowing many to act as if anything they do would not affect them. Our scientist tells us that everything in this world is interconnected, from the ecosystem, the weather, to the world's economy, and to the smallest particle. But many still ignore this fact and continue to live in their illusive reality.

Intellect is governed by Identity. Identity determines how the intellect will be used at any event. Intellect will create the logic to justify this identity. Some of us identify with a country, with a race, with a religion, a group or political party. All these will determine how we use our intellect and how we behave.

A recent movement happened in the world that was a great example of this. Many followers of this political movement identified themselves with the ideas and beliefs of its leaders. It made it acceptable to bring many destructive ideas and beliefs to the public. It made it possible for those with those ideas and beliefs to express themselves without guilt or shame. Intellect seemed to be the problem of this movement. Many attributed this movement to ignorance, bigotry and hate. Nevertheless, what created the problem was their identity, their beliefs and ideas about their reality and their lack of connection to others who might not belong to the ideals they so desperately try to identify with. Many of these people who were part of the movement believed to be attacked, abused, and many fear to be losing their national identity. They also hold the idea that other groups were unworthy of their country and sympathy. The leaders of this movement were the proof that intellect was not the problem, many of these men were very successful politicians, businessmen, and millionaires. A person needs to have some level of intellect to be successful at anything. Unfortunately, identity was dominating their intellect and many of their ideas were related to that identity. Therefore, their intellect was there to protect it. There are many other examples of men who have proof to have a high level of intellect, but behaved in a way that showed the contrary due to their identity problem.

Memory is the data that our body and mind have collected through experience, evolution, and genetics. This memory is in some cases the automatic function of the mind and body. The pumping of your heart is in your body's memory; your digestive system does all the work by using its evolutionary and genetic memory. Hunger, pain and other body functions that we experience in our daily lives are part of that memory. Going to sleep, setting up the clock and waking up every day in the morning is part of the mind's memory. This part of the mind does not require any thinking, any reasoning, or deliberation. Most of it is automatic, instinctive. Just like a great athlete or MMA fighter who memorizes every technique (a series of body movements) through constant practice and repetition. Athletes practice and practice their movements so that those movements become part of the minds and body's memory.

Intelligence is that which many refer to as consciousness, this is the basis of all the other three. Consciousness is the deepest level of the mind, is the substance of our reality. Consciousness is the state of being awake and aware of one's surroundings. This means living in a state of constant wakefulness, constant attention to every detail, every thought, word or deed we perform.

A conscious being is a person who is in total control of his/her mind and live. A person who lives in this high level of consciousness understands the power of thoughts, words and actions, therefore anything he/she does is well thought of, and well planned. Literally everything is done with purpose. They understand that everything they think, say, and do, has an effect in the physical reality. This type of awareness is required in every level of our lives, from something so simple as eating habits to something regarded as very important as a great scientific discovery or philosophical theory.

According to the ancient teachings from India, there are seven levels of consciousness in which all of us move through.

The first level of consciousness is related to survival instincts which are safety, security, and survival. Many have mastered this level of consciousness and have succeeded in securing their basic survival needs. We share this basic level to a certain level with the animal kingdom. All animals and even plants use this level of consciousness to survive and thrive. However, many people have taken this level to an extreme, causing others to have a difficult time meeting their basic survival needs.

The second level of consciousness is associated with well-being, pleasure, and sexuality. We share this level with the animal kingdom as part of the reproductive survival and preservation of the species.

The third level of consciousness is related to self-awareness and identity. Self-awareness and identity are subjects which many struggle with. Due to this struggle people are forced to find their identity in cults, groups, and religion. In this level, many suffer lack of self-esteem and self-worth. Many mistaken ideology and life goals with whom they truly are or want to be.

The fourth level of consciousness is connected to emotions such as love, passion, and fear. This level of consciousness is where we go to the more spiritual realm and less physical. In this level people tend to be more compassionate, and empathetic, but people can also experience anger, frustration, fear, and be emotionally disconnected.

The fifth level is linked to communication and self-expression. In this level, people can experience expression of inner wisdom, as well as over-opinionated and abusive ways of expression.

Creativity, imagination, critical thinking, and intuition are related to the sixth level of consciousness. At this level, human beings can experience success, peace, and a deep understanding of things.

The last level of consciousness is related to intelligence, and universal awareness. At this stage a human being can experience great wisdom, universal understanding, clarity, a universal sense of purpose, and the interconnection between oneself and the whole.

A conscious being is simply aware, attentive of his/her inner and outer surroundings and realities. A being with a high level of consciousness understands the connection of everything and everyone. This person understands that for every action there is a reaction. That there is a balance to everything in this universe. That the meaning of all is the meaning we chose. That all answers we seek are found within.

Thoughts on this chapter:
1. There are four basic levels of the mind; Intellect, Identity, Memory, and Intelligence.
2. Intelligence is also consciousness
3. Consciousness is the state of being awake, aware, attentive, and focused
4. There are seven levels of consciousness

Chapter 7: Spirituality

To put it in one phrase spirituality is to experience the world from the inside out. Spirituality is nothing more than the source of everything, it is the beginning and the end. Spirituality is what casts the shadow of the physical world. Without the Spiritual realities, the physical universe would cease to exist. The physical universe would have no sense, no purpose, no meaning, and no existence.

To better illustrate this idea, I would like you to imagine a toy in an infinite empty space, without a child or no one around to play with it, to see it, to experience it, to name it, to give it meaning. As you imagine this. Think of this scenario for a second and answer the following questions.

If there is no child or no one to play with the toy, then, what is the meaning or the purpose of that toy? Would that toy still be a toy without a child or no one around it?

If your answer is, yes, then why would you think so? Hence, you might need to ask yourself, what makes a thing a toy?

If your answer is, no, what happens to the toy then?

The answer to the first question is that the toy loses its meaning. The child is what makes a thing a toy. We see this in our everyday lives with children who are constantly making toys out of anything. Would you agree that children always find a way to make something a toy no matter what it is they will find a way to play with the thing, thus making the thing a toy?

The answer to the last question is that the toy without a child becomes NOTHING. The toy ceases to exist. There is no one to look at it, no one to play with it, no one to decide WHAT IT

IS. The toy becomes NOTHING. It never existed, it never was, and it will never be without a child or no conscious being around it. This truth is so simple and profound that the mind begs to ask, what does this mean?

Well, I will tell you this. The physical universe is like a toy.

If there were no self-conscious beings around the physical universe, the universe would be NOTHING. The physical universe is what it is because that is what self-conscious beings have made it to be. Just like a child has made a thing a toy. What this means to you is that consciousness is the true reality; consciousness is part of the spiritual reality. Consciousness is what gives meaning to things by simply being there.

Think of something that has great value today. Understand the reasons and the causes. What or who measures its value? What would happen to its value if the entire human race was removed overnight from the planet? I encourage you to do some research on this subject and truly dig deeper. One example I can use that comes to mind is money. What would happen to money if the entire human race was removed overnight from this planet?

In a scenario like this we can conclude that money will cease to exist, money and its value becomes nothing. We give it its current value and meaning.

What this tells us is that we the conscious beings give value and meaning to things. We also give meaning to events. Life is an event, and as such we give it meaning. We decide what it all means. Life is meaningless, it only means what we decide. All events in life mean nothing, except what we choose. We often ask ourselves, what is the meaning of life? And the answer to that question is found within us. All answers exist within. We are the ones who decide what the answer is.

This is where Spirituality comes into play, and this is how spirituality plays its part in our reality. Just as Jesus responded to the Pharisees according to the bible "the kingdom of God is within you" (Luke 17:20-21). This might be a difficult statement to understand for many, but the meaning of this statement is not literal. The confusion in many people about this statement is due to the general idea that the Kingdom of God is a place. When you think of the Kingdom of God in terms of a place then the statement makes no sense. How would a place be within us? That is not possible, right? But if we remove the idea of the Kingdom of God being a place and replace it with the idea that is more of a state of being. Then, we can better understand the statement. What this statement really means is that the Kingdom of God is not a place, but a state of being. Therefore, you can find the Kingdom of God within, because your state of being, your joy, your attitude, and your perspective, are within. No matter where we are in a state of Joy the Kingdom of God can be anywhere. Thus, the place is not important, what is important, is your state of being. Are you being Joyful or unjoyful?

You can be at a very beautiful place full of joy and peace, but if your inner being is in turmoil the place would not matter, you would still not be joyful nor peaceful. Many of us have experienced this at some point in our lives. Sometimes we go on a vacation to a beautiful place to relax and get away from our daily responsibilities and stresses, but we find ourselves still stressed out about money, work, health, or our family. We try to ignore all those things, and at some point, we succeed in forgetting momentarily by using external distractions, but we always come back to our reality. The truth cannot be hidden for long; therefore distractions are not the real and permanent solution to our worries.

Distractions are like the drug we take to relieve physical pain for a few hours but will never truly take the pain away. What this suggests is that distractions are not the permanent solutions to our pains.

Nonetheless, I am not suggesting that the kingdom of God is about ignoring the problems, to the contrary I suggest that to be at true peace and joy, we must recognize and accept our circumstances. We must understand the cause of the problem that is tormenting us and look within, so we can experience things from inside out and with a new outlook of things. This is the key to true peace, to true joy. Ignoring the problem will only lead to more worry and sorrow. Recognizing the problem will lead to finding the cause and a real permanent solution, thus finding true peace within.

Jesus truly lived up to his statement. He was peaceful and joyful most of his life. He died in the cross at peace of knowing that he was doing the will of the Father. He found the true meaning of experiencing life from within and not from without. He truly was a remarkable example of this. Jesus found the Kingdom of God within and kept it even to the final hours of His human life. His outlook of life came from his inner experience, He understood that he was in control, that he was a conscious being that gave meaning to things and events, and that his inner reality was the compass and map that would determine his external experience.

Therefore, look for your joy from within, not without. You will find permanent peace and joy within you. The Kingdom of God is truly within. Experience your reality from inside out.

Thus, I would like to summarize the four most important things from this chapter to help us keep focused on the subject.

1. We give meaning and value to things and events. We give meaning to life.
2. Without conscious beings anything physical or events will not have any purpose or meaning.
3. Spirituality is to experience all from within and not from without

PART 2: THE THREE DISCIPLINES

Chapter 8: The First Discipline - The Goal

The spiritual goal could be anything that has true meaning to you, anything that truly moves you, that truly represents you, that shows who you truly are.

What does that mean? You might ask.

Well, it means you can make your goal whatever you want, whatever has true meaning to you. That is spirituality. In a way if by this time you have not yet fully understood the concept of spirituality, you might want to simply make that your spiritual goal.

- UNDERSTAND SPIRITUALITY

Or better yet, experience it.

That is a good goal; that is a good place to start. If you can start with that as your first goal, you will soon reach it and begin with a new goal.

What would that goal be?

That is entirely up to you. You will decide your next step. You will decide if you want to continue or stay where you are, is all up to you. Nevertheless, for many people this is difficult, because most people want someone else to tell them where to go. I am not here to tell you where to go, I'm here to tell you that is up to you to find out.

All answers you seek are within you. The Kingdom of God is within. Look into your experience and think about your options and opportunities. This exercise requires some deep thinking; it will take time and effort, but the journey will be worth an eternity.

The truths that you can find in the inner reality are so valuable that your world will change in an instant and forever. You will change dramatically, once you see this new inner reality. Do not look within with your eyes, look within with your mind. This inner reality exists in the thought plane, it has no color, no shape, no smell, and no sound. This reality is out of reach of the five physical senses. This reality is not made of anything physical, therefore you cannot find it the same way you would find your keys. Looking within means looking into your thoughts, your ideas, your values, your beliefs, your perspective, your attitude, your paradigms, your character, your intellect, your identity, your memory, your consciousness, your awareness. These are the levels of the inner reality that I'm pointing you to. Levels, which unfortunately many ignore and do not understand. My attempt is to point you in the right direction and give you some guidance in where to look, but the rest of the journey is up to you. You must put effort into exploring a new frontier that only those with great patience, determination, curiosity, wonder, and love would look for.

For those who have found this inner world have found great joy, peace, and understanding. To those who have experience and practice the inner truths of the universe and themselves have found a purpose. They have found the ultimate purpose and understand it with great joy.

The Second Discipline – Lead Measures

Here is the other hard part of this exercise. The next step is to define the lead measures or habits that will take you there. Think about the things you can do that will help you reach your goal, be creative, and be specific. There are millions of possibilities, options and habits that you can adopt and change as you see them fit. I will show some examples so that you can use them as a point of reference. Everyone has different needs and wants. This is just an example, therefore use it as such.

- Read more about spirituality
- Asks someone
- Ask yourself
- Ask your highest self.
- Meditate about it daily

The way to define your spiritual goal is up to you. I can only make suggestions or give you some ideas about what your spiritual goal is, and what habits will take you there.

The idea is that you start somewhere, you start NOW. Do not let time pass by. The time to do something different, to change the world, to change ourselves, is now. Any attempt to change the world without changing ourselves is completely futile. Our inward must change to change the outward. All truth, all realities, all changes start from within.

The Third Discipline – Reconcile

The next step is to reconcile.

Reconcile your actions, be truthful to yourself and look at the things that you are doing one by one and see if they are truly taking you to your goal. The idea is that you look, discern, compare, and examine your actions.

The questions to ask are.
1. Is this action taking me to where I want to go?
2. Is this getting me closer?
3. Or at the very least, have I taken any action?

If you do not take action, it will be as if you never moved, neither towards nor away from your goal. You had basically stayed in the same place. Therefore, take action, do not be afraid, but do not forget to reconcile. Make sure you look at the direction that the action is taking you, and then make your assessment. If necessary, make the changes that will take you where you want to go. This is a very important step that cannot be missed or ignored. Our failure to take this last step could lead away from our goal and bring great frustration during the process.

Chapter 9: Why?

You might ask why you are doing this. Well, the answer is very simple.

Because you are looking for the truth, you are looking for inner peace. Why else? You are looking for yourself, the ultimate meaning, the ultimate reality.

You are seeking the truth, because what you have found so far is not enough. What you know now is not serving you; it's not helping you; it's not working for you. So, you came here to find a way, a new way, a different way to live, to find purpose.

You are looking for a new way to make sense of it all, to find answers, to find truth. I will tell you this. The truth is within you, and I'm merely pointing you there. Pointing you in the direction you can find the truth, YOUR TRUTH. Your purpose is also within you, just as your truth.

However, this is not the only way to find truth, inner peace is only one of many ways. So, if this does not work for you, do not worry, there are many other ways, just keep looking. Look within you, just as I did and many before me. There are many masters that are here to help us find our way, look for them too, you might be able to find another method that will bring you to your grandest goal.

This is just like going to Chicago. Depending on where you are standing relative to Chicago, there are many ways you can get there. The same goes for your truth. YOUR TRUTH is even better, is bigger than Chicago, you cannot miss it, you just must look. Open your eyes; open your mind; open your SOUL.

Why else?

Because this can take you to your true happiness, to your true calling.

Why else?

Maybe, you might have the answer. That answer is within YOU. Only you have that answer. No one can answer that for you. This might be depressing for some, but you should rejoice to know that you have the power to choose. The power to control everything in your life and your experience. No one has to tell you, no one is in charge of your life but you.

Chapter 10: The Sample

The 3 disciplines of Spirituality

Spiritual Goal

a. Define Who You Truly Are

Lead Measures

1. Meditate and repeat to yourself daily 'I AM A MASTER OF LIFE'.
2. Every thought, word or deed needs to represent Who You Really Are.
3. Be Grateful, Loving, Accepting, Joyful, and Blessing
4. Have a conversation with God
5. Serve others
6. Listen twice as much as you speak
7. Have wisdom, love, firmness, and self-control in any situation
8. Begin the day with an end in mind
9. These roles take priority in achieving my mission
    a. Husband – my partner is the most important person in my life. Together we contribute the fruits of harmony, charity, and love.
    b. Father – I help my children experience progressively greater joy in their lives.
    c. SON/BROTHER – I am frequently "there" for support and love
    d. Spiritual – To serve others and seek to be the best that I can be.

e. Change agent – I am a catalyst for developing high performance in large organizations

   f. Scholar – I learn important new things every day

Reconcile

1. Every Moment reconcile with every action, thought, and word and compare to see if they represent Who You Really Are

2. Act over any action, thought, or word that does not represent Who You Really Are, and make a new and better decision, thought, and word.

This is only an example of what I have used for myself, and I want to clarify that you do not necessarily have to use the same goal, and lead measures. Instead use this as a base for your spiritual goal, for your own disciplines. However, if this fits what you are looking for, then go ahead and use it, have fun with it, play with it, change it, and improve it.

The idea is that you start somewhere, as you go along you might change it, you might make it better.

www.ingramcontent.com/pod-product-compliance
Lightning Source LLC
LaVergne TN
LVHW040202080526
838202LV00042B/3287